Minding My
Ps & Qs

Poems and Quotes

R.E. Leyland

authorHOUSE®

AuthorHouse™
1663 Liberty Drive
Bloomington, IN 47403
www.authorhouse.com
Phone: 1 (800) 839-8640

Published by AuthorHouse 08/09/2019

ISBN: 978-1-7283-2259-9 (sc)
ISBN: 978-1-7283-2258-2 (e)

Library of Congress Control Number: 2019911480

Print information available on the last page.

This book is printed on acid-free paper.

Dedication

Dedicated to my loving wife and my two beautiful boys.

Poems

*T*he following expressions were my early efforts at incarnating the interior of my being. The crafting of my poetry one might say. A time when I was very young in all aspects. But one must start somewhere and here is where I began...in the years of 1986 thru 1988...*The Early Years.*

She'll Never Be Mine

*O*nce we were friends then we tried something new,
We planted a kiss in the dark.
When it began I thought nothing of it-love's misdemeanor
But as time progressed I grew to crave this affection I never knew.
An affection infected by you that you were making come true.
It was in the peak of our wanting one another that we became insecure.
Time tells and here is what it told of us.
While my heart grew more "in love" with you
Your heart diminished with love for me.
Unexpectedly you were gone, without reason or explanation.
It was then that questions and confusion dominated my brain
Beseeching answers for my wonder why this time had came.
I am left now ever haunted by the stilled photo
Of you that suspends on a wall
– so near and yet so far out of reach.
The ghostly effigy of a haunting memory
That painfully conveys to me...
She'll never be mine.

Thinking Time

*I*t is now the Thinking Time
When the silence is loud
And wandering eyes are stood still.
That moment wherein inquiring minds ask many questions
Questions that search for many answers
Answers that sometimes come
And sometimes not.

Many moods are felt, many thoughts are thought
In the presence of Thinking Time.
Many fantasies spawn, deep captivated desires
Surface in the cauldron of Thinking Time.
Thinking Time makes for sad eyes when over-
Love is recalled – when images of the past
Come flooding back, when the poison of
Yesterday's choices infects with regret.
Oh that the past might be forgotten when forgetting
Is not an option in the Thinking Time.
Here again, our psyche-fiend preys upon a by himself-man.
Here in a park, lost in the dark
Fist on face, elbow on thigh, looking but not seeing the people go by.
Then there is he, a boy in bed lost inside his own head
Embarrassed by a hurtful yesterday, a dreadful
Tomorrow and a wasted today.
Close your eyes and lullaby away the mind's angst
Fortifying against enough of the brain's pranks...
Mind, mind let me be
Your Thinking Time is killing me.

The Unfortunate One

No one but You Lord can hear his cry
From his darken empty room
Where he is learning to live without love.
There have been many a nights
He lay on his bedroom floor
Listing to the music he adores;
Songs that helped him feel he wasn't alone.
Other nights he would dress for an evening,
Then realize, 'why should I care what I wear
When this night will be like all my nights,
A night not shared for The Unfortunate One?'
He knows he's loved,
But not in this corner of the world.
He feels wanted,

But not in this corner of the world.
He is talked about,
But not in this corner of the world.
In this corner of the world,
He is The Unfortunate One.
If you think him to be handsome, good-
looking, or simply appeals to you,
Let him know.
If you think him to be nice, kind or charming,
Please let him know.
Because he'll never know if you never tell him,
And I think you would like him,
If only you could meet him,
If only you knew him.
There have been days when he walked alone in a crowd
Singing lyrics for the world to hear
And sadden by the fact that God was his only listener.
One day he will return to that corner of the world
Where he feels wanted and loved,
Where he may not be The Unfortunate One.
But until then and for now, he is here
Where The Unfortunate One is him,
And I am him
The Unfortunate One.

Questioning The Answer

Mamma, why has life gott'n me so down?
Would it be better if I wasn't around?
I know it's sad to say those words
But if they're true let them be said.
I'm killing myself with my choice to be sad,
That sadness that has become my dominating emotion.
Mamma, does true love exist between a man and woman?
If so, is it something I'll ever know?

My Wants I Fear

I see it all around me, people claiming they're "in love."
What is love?
It doesn't appear that they know.
She loves him while he loves another.
He loves her while his her loves a different him.
Love's lovers seem to lose more than they win.
Love's fear is not love-itself but love's end.
Is this the fruit of love?
Eden's apple eaten-leaving naiveté lovers vulnerably condemned?
Is this the destination of my soul's hopes and longings?
If so, I want it no more.
It hurts to much this thing called "love"
If love be that which I see.
Hurt upon hurt makes me fear love.
Beauty upon beauty makes me desire love.
I surmise that the heart must be kept from love's web
If I want to keep my mind from love's asylum.
My wants I fear-tis such a shame.
My wants I fear – tis my pain.
I fear what I want and it's my endless game.

*T*he following expressions were composed during the 90s – during a time of inner turmoil and civil unrest (within myself that is). These poems were my attempt at "working-things-out." I'll title these poems *The 90s.*

8/27/94

I, Discipline contend with Compulsion and lose.
I, Compulsion come and go but when I come I control.
When I control I take hold of saints and sinner alike.
By My commands, puppets submit to my puppeteer hands
Forgoing integrity for foolish en-slavery.
Once I, Compulsion am done having My fun
I transfer My slave to Self-Condemnation.
Then I, Self-Condemnation confuse, accuse, judge and misuse
The prey given away who has no say.
By the power of My might
I, Self-Condemnation further flog with isolation and shame
Making wrong them who deemed themselves "right."
In such vulnerable disposition I, Hopelessness take my position
And come in to oppose hope and life itself.
Sometimes I win – sometimes I flee to fight another day.
Then there's I, Grace that holds dominion to trump all
If chosen to be used by those who call.
I, Grace hold the power to restore
The Fallen and those labeled "abhorred."
To bring back to life those who've sinned not-unto-death
With unlimited forgiveness and love that forgets.

1/12/96 – Broken Bird

*N*o bird can possibly fly when a wing is broken.
No matter the strength of the instinctual drive to fly
The wound will seal the fate of the bird's flight.
I am a bird. That bird. Wounded, broken-winged bird.
I who once flew high now descend downward –

Wounded, broken, plummeting to the Earth
To crawl in replacement of my soaring.
Folly for wisdom. Prostration for elation.
It is though I give in to defeat.
On the verge of waving my white flag of surrender.
Yet I still have this hope;
My tomorrows will save me from my todays
And reclaim what the locust has eaten of my yesterdays.
I am a broken bird in need of healing.

9/8/96 – I Am...Because I Am Not...

I am foolish because I am not wise.
I am wrong because I am not right.
I am white because I am not black.
I am guilty because I am not innocent.
I am mortal because I am not immortal.
I am alive because I am not dead.
I am ignorant because I am not smart.
I am slow because I am not fast.
I am old because I am not young.
I am thin because I am not fat.
I am insane because I am not sane.
I am lost because I am not found.
I am fake because I am not real.
I am weak because I am not strong.
I am scared because I am not courageous.
I am here because I am not there.
I am etc... because I am not....
I am what I am because of all the things
I am not.

9/30/96 – Aging

*T*he light of heaven has set once again
Behind the western edge,
A little earlier now
Escorting in the night a little sooner.
Summer is having its last stand
And in the twinkle of an eye
I will live in fall and the anticipation of the coming winter.
Seasons come and they must go
While the descending sands of time
Turn boys in to men.
Cracks appear on the smooth surface face
That were never there before.
The agile-invincible body
Now begins to have its aches.
The Hawk-eyes grow dim,
Taking away organic clarity
Morphing in to optical obscurity.
Childhood hopes and dreams
Are vanquished and obliterated
By adulthood roles
And an existence that is regimented.
If God shall will
I shall live for the duration of another year
And another year to follow – if God shall will.
But what difference will there be for me?
Shall I live with the hope that age will bring to
Fruition the dreams of my youth?
Or do I make things happen with the understanding
Of risks within every potential?
And/or, does an answer even matter?
Seasons represent change.
My cracked face, my hairless head and aching anatomy
Are the fruits of an inevitable process that happens to all: Aging.
Age is seasons coming and going,
The sun rising and setting
Without the power to disrupt or halt the motion of impermanence.

Why fight what cannot be won? Why contend
With what cannot be fought?
Accept this truth: youth is but a vapor, one blow and we are old.
Hello seasons. Goodbye youth.

6/13/97

I am down. Low down.
Life is but a daze, a haze, a maze
I am ill-equip to navigate in.
I have wronged.
A self-made culprit.
I ache. My heart is blue.
My existence is without vitality.
I know myself to be a child of life
While suffering the pangs of a living death.
Contradiction? Or Paradox? Either/or? And/both?
Being-in-pain is the answer to all posed questions.
I am down. Low down.
Wondering who I am
And ever exhausted from existence.

1/1/98

I dream a dream like Fantine.
I walk alone like Eponine.
I struggle with the psyche of Claude Frollo.
"Master of my domain" is something I do not know.
I lay tortured on the iron maiden of my own making,
Veiling a mortal heart that lives in a constant state of breaking.
Tormented within an isolated cell,
Cursed by an unbreakable spell
That descends my soul in an icy hell,
Hearing the tolling of a thousand knells.
Banished to a labyrinth of a lonely abyss,
Plagued by the desires for a stranger's kiss.

In youth I was pierced by Cupid's Golden Arrow
And without a Daphne, love is but an existence of sorrow.

1/10/98 – Costly Conformity Creed

*W*hat hearts that bleed
Through webs we weave
From masks we wear to please.
What conflicts repressed
Through social jest
Making acceptance the golden quest.
What countenance turn pale
When the God-like fail
Appalled by the poison that extracts from Holy Grail.
What Jekyll's we present
In order to pay rent
For a space at the human circus tent.
What Hyde's are concealed
In attempts to reveal
An appearance of unity at the harmony meal.
What human may die
Although still alive
Suppressing a truth to live out a lie.

7/5/98 – The Unanswered Question – Where Were You?
(Holocaust)

*W*here were You when evil reigned?
Why so silent during Jewish pain?
When children's smiles were burned away
By a diabolical plan, by a Fuhrer's flame.
Where were Your ears when Abraham's children screamed?
When concentration camps killed more than just dreams.
Where were You when Your people cried?
When the incarnate devil attempted genocide.
Where were You when healthy bodies evolved in to living bones?

When joyous expressions became lifeless stones.
Where were You when hell came to earth?
When the stench of death replaced the aroma of mirth.
Where were You when lullabies turned in to living nightmares?
When the Nazi epidemic forced humans in to barbed wire and despair.
Now, a memorial of motionless horror stands in black and white
Reminding us of the visitation of terror and of one people's plight.
On behalf of the six million and those who were set free
Remains an unanswered question that often baffles me.
When darkness prevailed and a serpent's bite made spirits bleed
Where were You in the midst of all this,
Omnipotent God of eternity?

8/20/98 – Vicious Cycle

*H*ow can one blame you Lord for refusing to use a wretched person?
One who continually returns to behaviors vowed to never return to?
Those compulsive behaviors that erodes away acquired integrity.
Oh the Vicious Cycle...
Contend.
Give in.
Plan.
Seek.
Obtain.
Consume.
Am consumed.
Fall.
Regret.
Repent.
Promises made.
Restored.
Born Again.
...only for a span of time before the giving in comes again
And the wretched man contends.

9/25/98

O'detrimental curiosity, thou art ever present
In the idle mind vexed with boredom.
How vulnerable thou art when the witching hour arises
And temptation beckons for the surrender of mortal desires.
"Succumb, succumb." Is the mandate of the Siren
Who lures with deceitful red lips,
Igniting the hellish fire that burns for the forbidden fruit of Eden.
She is but a sensual idol that breeds the sons and heirs of vulgar vice.
They who surrender to her enticing guile
Drink unto themselves the cup of hemlock
And die the death of Juliet.
They who resist her seduction
Only repress her into the concealed caverns of their psyche
And are left to struggle to function
While living with the madness of Ophelia.
Such is the state of ordinary man
Who is tortured by the voodoo of sheer perfection
That incarnates itself in the figure of a woman.

2/19/99

*D*earest Lord,
Surely the man whose sin is forgiven is blessed,
But truly the man who does not sin is most blessed.
Show me such a man – he who is without sin?
For he – she – we – them – they-all sin
For ALL sin and fall short.
Wherein lay the hope Dearest Lord?
In covenant Mercy and covenant Grace
Contingent on Your character and Your character alone.
For Your mercy taketh away
And Your grace giveth.
Atonement and Heaven – both by You and You alone.
There can be no human citizenship in God's Kingdom
But by and through God and God alone.

Blessed are all whose transgressions are forgiven,
Whose sins are covered.
Simply accredited...A mercy that endureth forever
And an amazing grace that is eternally sufficient.

4/26/99-Sadie's Sorrow (Tiny Dancer)

*Y*ou can call her Sadie
That's her occupational name.
The one she uses
In her four-walled domain.
Blood-red lips
And a welcoming smile.
Her figure in motion
Intended to drive customers wild.
Eyes of seduction
Design to lure you in.
Abandoning conviction
Surrendering to sin.
She'll make you feel special
For the right price.
Blinded by the guile
Even believing "Sadie's pretty nice."

She is called Sadie
But she knows that's not her name.
It's the one she's chosen
To cover her internal pain.
Customers come and customers go
Not caring for Sadie, just wanting a show.
Just an objectified image
For men to behold.
A soaked up glacier
That stands frozen and alone.

Deep inside Sadie is a silent scream
A child of old who once had a dream.

A woman who hungers for love and affection
Whose life is turned towards another direction.
A lady of creativity whose heart yearns to bleed
The blood-of-love that all humans need.

I've called her Sadie
Though I know it's not her name.
I've paid for her company
In her four-walled domain.
I have used her
And she has used me.
In that captive atmosphere
Where neither one of us is free.

Once Sadie had shown me
Something new
A cavern in her heart
That knows only blue.
A woman of sorrow
Full of silent cries.
Screaming for help
In a world of lies.
A beautiful lady
Who hides behind Sadie.

You can call her Sadie
Though that's not her name.
It's her external mask
That hides all her shame.
You pay for smile
You pay for her eyes.
You pay for false affection
You pay for a lie.

Customers will continue to come
Today and tomorrow.
Purchasing time with Sadie
Without ever knowing the concealed woman of sorrow.

5/13/99

*M*oments should not be contaminated by imposing
Upon them meanings of trajectory.
Allow them – let them stand on their own – ends-unto-themselves.
Not needing to be qualified or disqualified
By predications of whether or not
They are part of a bigger whole.
"This moment means this" – Not –
"What does this moment mean?" – Or –
"What meaning should we make of this moment?"
May each and every moment stand on its own
Lived in for what it is…
A given moment to be experienced in
Not defined from.

*Y*es...what would poems be without Courtly Love? What would poetry be without the illusion of the Romantic Solution with its hopes of love and the tragedy of its loss? And what would the poet be without Eros? The following expressions where my efforts of articulating love hoped and love lost. Simply titled... **Love Sonnets.**

One Imaginative Night (Immanent-Love)

*I*magine if you could.
Imagine if you would.
A night. A granted night.
A night granted.
Grant me that night,
An evening wherein all other existence is blurred, irrelevant.
Permit our histories, our futures
To be consumed by a transcended presence,
An unbelievable here-and-now.
Yesterdays do not matter.
Tomorrows may never be.
It is only tonight that life resides in our beings –
Therefore let the descending sands of time freeze –
Let Zeus hold back the goddess of Dawn
And demand that Helios refrain from riding his chariot of fire
So as to contain the light of Heaven and prevent it
From ushering in the Day and scattering the Night.
And let us live as the only existing earthen creatures
Who possess the breath of life
And have been called by Fate
To pour that life in to one another.
The time is now.
For beyond your tranquil eyes
I see the potential beauty of a repressed soul
Tormented by un-embodied imagination.
RELEASE IT!
FREE IT!
Open your dreams and allow me to be your dream catcher,

Dream maker, dream filler.
Touch my immanent presence and know I am here.
I am now.
Fear me not. For I am not an apparition-
Nor spell nor omen.
Just a vulnerable mortal
Whose soul beckons for yours to come.
Do not think tonight –
Become existential and experience.
Live sensually and feel.
Holistically and live.
Defy the imposed laws of others.
Heed-not the pricking of the conscience.
Release yourself from the hemming-in of rational thinking
And surrender to the beseeching of your emotions.
The time is now. I am now. We are now.
For the night – this night
Belongs to the passionate souls
Who have been imprisoned by the shackles of immature choices.
Allow your senses the freedom they crave.
Give them liberty or die.
Trust them to my words, my touch, my breath.
Be ever so attentive to the sound of my human frailty
That extracts from the depths of my darken heart.
Succumb to the point of no return.
Permit the possibility of wonder
To lure you beyond the point of rescue.
Yes, be captive by the apparel of articulation –
Yes, you are captivated by my utterance.
Even though you try to resist, you grow weary
Like a pedal of a rose trying to hold the weight of the morning dew.
Why fight what cannot be beaten?
You cannot win.
Eloquence of speech ravages your senses
Making you aware that all your hidden fantasies
Are at the fingertips of reality.
You are lost in the allure of passion
And yet you've never felt so found.

No need to shiver. No need to tremble.
What you are experiencing is the pure fruit of unveiled souls
That are becoming naked in the arena of honesty.
It's the place where the garments of restricted reality are abolished
And replaced by the incarnation of primal-oriented dreams.
Freedom...freedom...freedom
Is the yearning of our souls
And tonight – this night
The gods have granted us emancipation
From the bondage of our regimented restrictions,
That we may experience the passion that has been held back for years.
But only for tonight.
This night. A granted night.
A night granted.
NO! NO! Cupid!
I demand that your arrow have no part in this enticement.
Her soul must come on its own volition.
I will have it no other way!
There can be no mortal passion from a soul
Spellbound by a love potion from the gods.
Two souls must be entwined as a result of willful vulnerability.
Not the entrapment of novelty.

Alive

Sometimes it only takes the tone of a musical note.
Sometimes the touch of another's skin.
Sometimes a particular look from a particular set of eyes
To reverberate, amplify, make alive
The dormant essence that resides inside.
To stir once again the subjugated being
That is no longer beheld
But rather held, confined, concealed
In the shadows of some prescribed reality.

Harp

A stilled-silent harp
Is a disservice to the essence of its beauty.
Plucking and caressing of its strings
By the skillful lover of its beauty
Vibrates the outlet of its fullness.
There and then
The fullness of its beauty is expressed.

The Butterfly Collector (The Spider and the Butterfly)

I love every new butterfly I see
That flies in my eye and elicits the hunter in me.
Spawning the net that aims to capture thee
And you my dear are the latest intrigue I see
Fluttering and flying around me.
Enchanted, spellbound I be
By the mystery, the muse of thee
That ignites and inspires the poetry.
Curvaceous anatomy
With wings of splendor tapestry
Soaring around while never landing on me –
Awakening within primal biology
With unarticulated ecstasy and imploded agony.
So passionately I chase to selfishly take the you that is free
That I might pin and mount for me the fullness of your alluring artistry.

The Magical Room In A Private Universe

There is a movie in my mind that plays and plays and plays.
It shows continual scenes that cannot be erased.
There is a room that dwells in a private universe.
Its walls are made of safety.
Its foundation is authentic vulnerability.
It's fragranced with the aroma of intimate passion.

There are two who occupy the room.
Only these two know of its existence.
It is they who blindly created the room
With the tools of accumulated magical moments.
A curious one sparked curiosity in the other
And they both gave birth to an unacceptable beauty.
They knew it was wrong
But could not forsake what felt so right.
Every meeting was to be their last
But passion beckoned them to return to one another –
Again and again and again.
She was beautiful.
Her eyes showed a side of her that was never revealed prior.
Those eyes cried, they gleamed, they hypnotized,
They were honest and they captivated him.
Her lips were soft.
They transferred the expressions of her heart.
They were hypnotically magnetic and he was pulled in to them.
Her skin was silk.
When she wore her hair up it manifested the beauty of her neck
And the sensual scent of her body could nearly be tasted.
Resistance was ever futile.
He had to caress her tangible beauty that was ever present.
They were dreamers making a titillating dream come true.
They wrote a living romance novel.
They sang their own love song.
They lived out what others only dare to dream out.
Then came the end – they and their dream.
Today the two live in two different worlds –
Separate worlds – worlds apart.
Nevertheless, he returns to the memories of yesterday's passion plays,
Knowing the torturous pleasure he encounters when peering through
The ajar door of what was and no longer is.
Ever still, no matter the distance time accumulates between the two,
There will always exist a magical room in a private universe
Where in a piece of two became one heart that time cannot divide.

Objectified

*T*ruly I have objectified you.
I have made you more than your subjectivity will ever let you be.
In fact, the more I encounter your subjectivity
The less I like you.
It's in the objectifying of you that my desires were born and fanned.
I actually anger towards your subjectivity.
It comes against what my objectification has made you out to be –
The object that I want – that I desire –
The object your subjectivity won't allow me to have.
I don't want to see, I don't want to know
The subjective you.
I want to experience the objective you that I've objectified.
My hope is that the subjective you
Will become the objective you that I've created you to be.
The objectified you I've made for me.

Hot-Ice

*Y*ou're fragile
Like china in my arms.
You're erotic
As one who possesses a charm.
You spellbind me
With your gentleness.
I am mesmerized by your sculpture
I crave to nakedly caress.
You are the goddess of my idolatry
The object of my desire.
You are a distant glacier
That fuels my darken fire.
Your sensations are aroused
By the simplicity of a kiss.
Potions of endearment flow
Through the clashing of our lips.
My fingers pluck you

Like that of a skilled musician.
Concealing your eyes from seeing
Your body takes on new conditions.
Paralyzed by the pleasure of a
Moistness that comes
From the words of a soul
That voluntarily succumbs
To a tabooed pleasure
That continues to grow
Because of a weakened will
That refuses to say "no."
Our moments of magic
Are so far and few
Making all other minutes of existence
Torturous blue.

Life's Spice...flavors

I have loved many-a-women in my life.
A love defined by me...of myself.
A love that risks the scrutiny, a judgement, even a condemning
Coming from a nebulous definition of love
As though Love were a floating-invisible-Platonic-Ideal
To be lived up to – to be loved into.
I am unconcerned by those who would question
whether I have loved or not.
I know I have loved and have loved many
and imagine loving many more;
Whatever that love for many has been, is and will be
Is a love that has been, is and will be qualified by me.
Unconventional? Unorthodox? Unethical?
Nevertheless...
Unconfined! Uninhibited! Unlimited!
Holistically Fluid...Holistic Fluidity.
You think what you will.
I'll experience all that I feel.
You speculate.

I'll know.
You deny and conceal
I'll show and grow.
I have been pricked by many a-thorns
While delighting in the roses bloom.
I have been scorched and charred
While interplaying with Venus's perfume.
Par for one's duty to beauty.
The bitter and the sweet.
The beauty and the beast.
Still I have known:
Dark Chocolate to Coco-Bean.
Rising Sun to Whipped Cream.
From local Licorice to International Blend.
From Cross Pollinating to Jungle-Fever-Mating.
Just Love...Divine...of my own...Defined.
Nothing more! Certainly nothing less!
Not purely altruistic but highly intrinsic.
Fully intentional and completely edible.
This was, is and shall be my duty...a disciple of beauty.

Spanish Fly

O Spanish eyes
How you've mesmerized, hypnotized, took me by surprise.
O Spanish lips
I'm forced to resist, aching to taste their gentle kiss.
O Spanish smile
Igniting my guile, making me vulnerable like that of a child.
O Spanish hair
Captured my glare, let it rest on my chest as an expression of care.
O Spanish skin
Soft and thin, concealing much that is shackled within.
O Spanish name
Rekindled my flame, bringing with it the lover's pain.
O Spanish woman
Skillfully woven, by the gods of Olympus the earth has now stolen.

O Spanish spell
Making my heart swell, with potions of passion that yearn to tell.
O Spanish soul
Empty and cold, the one I had touched but could not hold.
O Spanish eyes
Making me cry, fighting a reality we attempt to deny.
O Spanish Fly
Forget not my eyes, the one who brought your hungry soul alive.

Life Unloved Is Life Unlived

To live is to love
And I shall live
If it be you that I love.
Life be but dreadful
Tis be not life at all
If life were to be lived
Without you
Life were to be lived
Without love.
Someone tell me
What good a garden wherein no rose blooms?
What value the East if no yonder light breaks?
Why stare into the West if there be no sunset?
Why strive to live if living be without you?
I shall die a thousand deaths a day
If it be to you I cannot say
"Love you I do."
Reality now comes true
I must live without love
Because I must live without you.
And all that remains is I,
Life's unlived lovesick fool.

Prisoned Poet

*W*hen heighten sensations are unexpressed
They fade away and die.
They become the womb that gives birth
To the walking dead inside.
I strive to be dedicated to reality
But in truth, life is but a lie.
I'm locked in a prison of unarticulated Eros
That yearns to flow to you.
I ache to touch your image
Even at the price of being a fool.
I cannot explain why I do what I do
I just know that my senses long to be tantalized by you.
Would you deprive a hungry boy who was in need of food?
Would you forsake the solving of a mystery by withholding a clue?
Would you laugh at a man who was feeling blue?
Then why must you withhold from me all that I desire of you?
Forgive me for be selfish and only thinking of me
I've opened Pandora's Box not knowing what I would see,
Narcissistic eyes only behold scenes of you and me.
Now my reality has become shadows in light of my fantasies,
Rational capacity is abandoned in the struggle for sanity
And you alone hold the key that would unlock
My imprisoned passions free
The passions that can only be known to you from me.

A Blasphemous Beauty (Escape from Freedom)

*B*iology is beautiful.
Your beauty is in your biology
But ever incarcerated and hidden behind your morality.
Beauty like yours
Should be owned and shown with fluidity
But yours is chained and suffocated by an empty piety.
What beauty –
What God given design you hold

That lurks in the shadow of your pious light
That can't be experienced nor expressed
Due to constructs defined by wrongs and rights.
Verily, verily I say, I loathe your religiosity
That lassoes the beauty of your biology
Ever so restricting my nefarious curiosity.
Rip the veil from your temple and split it asunder
So that the ontology of your beauty be freed
That others such as I could behold and have
And even you be made weak in the knees.
Let the sinner in me
Come boldly to the throne of your beauty
And pay the rightful homage to your anatomy.
Destroy the temple
Of your man-made rigidity
And resurrect the temple of your body's divinity.
Stretch forth your scepter and open wide your gates
That this Gentile may enter in to your holy of holies
And present offerings in to your sacred space.
Please do unto me as I would do unto you
And tear off the wineskins-of-old
And reveal the wineskins-of-the-new
So I can drink and be drunk off the wine of you.
Your beautiful biology is being lost to your religious mythology
And there's nothing I can do to get to the true beauty of you.
It saddens me...maddens me to state
That you're a jarred Quaintrelle and freedom is what you escape.

Illusionary Romeo

*W*ere it in my power
I would love thee until the dawn.
Access to a mutual night
I would be your Don Juan.
An exotic love
That knoweth not limitations
Making you the recipient of my erotic deprivations.

Two passionate people
Lost in their own sea,
Voyagers sailing
In constant ecstasy.
YET;
Utter misery is the body
That cannot touch the imagery of the mind.
Thou art a treasure I know of,
A treasure not permitted to find.
I am but a Montaque,
Thou but a Capulet.
I would be thy Romeo,
Thy will not be my Juliet.
Now the bitter pill of reality
Is mine to swallow slow,
As I look at my La Esmeralda
Through the distant eyes of Quasimodo.
Left to live in a silent woe,
Forever yours,

An Illusionary Romeo

Quotes

*T*he following quotes – my quotes – are not in any kind of particular order. Not divided up by theme, genre, or time. I simply just transferred them from the book I wrote them in to this typed text. They are my composition of random word-collaborations that spontaneously sprouted up within my brain over the period of 2007 till present.

*F*reedom is the ability to live in the gray.

I take Nature for granted and yet yearn to have
an intimate relationship with Her.

I want to cry sometimes because I am moved by things
that are forces beyond description and explanation.

*J*ust because someone is overly sensitive
does not make me insensitive.

*P*oisoned perceptions based on ignorant assumptions.

*L*ife is too short to be vague.

A deprived ego will gorge itself into an over-inflated ego.

I need the fortitude just to be.

*T*he personification of Zen is my child.

*L*ife is a quest to find what we lost through experience.

*I*f nothingness is everything then why does it
take everything to give up anything?

*L*ife is like a horserace-we run around in circles
and end up back where we started.

*T*he world is full of spineless gardeners who waste their
energies and other's time beating around the bush.

*A*n inch of possibility to a deprived soul is a foot of certainty.

*O*ne does not perceive what one sees; one sees what one perceives.

*C*uriosity is easier to combat then memory; memory
comes with contingencies of experience; curiosity
only has the influence of speculation.

I think; therefore I am neurotic.

*A*cceptance of incompleteness is the first step towards completeness.

*B*itter-sweet is the fatalistic pill that the human creature is forced to choke on.

*A*bility without opportunity leads to futility.

*W*e negate what is for what could be.

*W*isdom is knowledge actualized.

*D*on't say: Do
don't think: Be.

*D*on't go to bat for people who've taken a bat to you.

*T*o be lovable is endearing:
to be loving is attractive.

*F*amiliar lips breed desires for a stranger's kiss.

*G*ive me sticks and stones that break my bones
rather than words that kill me.

I am the author of my son's childhood memories.

*Y*outh projects the future:
age reflects the past.

*E*ach round determines the quality of the workout.

*T*he kiss of a stranger can be more arousing then sex with a familiar.

*L*augh more:
analyze less.

I'd rather be slapped in the face then stabbed in the back.

*C*hildren don't speak quieter:
they just whisper louder.

*B*etter a completed garden then pieces of a potential empire.

*M*ediocrity breeds boredom whereas the
forbidden makes life worth living.

*P*eople are like driveways:
some have cracks.

*K*nowledge is about doing:
wisdom is about being.

*A*ttachments to the potential are as powerful
as attachments to the actual.

*P*aradise is a good parking spot.

A badly fed deprivation can result in unhealthy expectations.

*E*xpect nothing:
be open to anything.

*L*ife should be a black spot on the Sun at its worse:
not a lighthouse in the dark at its best.

*M*ortal quest for omnipotence ends in human impotence.

*T*urning a blind-eye helps me see clearer.

*F*reedom without boundaries leads to bondage.

*H*ell hath no exists other then back-tracking
through the entrance which one hath made.

*S*leep provides pieces of peace:
pieces of peace are provided in sleep.

*O*ptions obscure rarity.

*I*f seeing was needed to accomplish the task:
then how would one ever wipe his own ass?

*E*nlightenment is regaining the innocence lost through higher learning.

*G*ood sleep is the antidote for a bad day.

*I*f not for music sometimes I would be without companionship:
if not for books sometimes I would be without intellectual conversa-
tions.

*O*nly heaven can accurately repay what loving-caring
parents have invested in to their children.

*A*ny training that excludes sparring is ill-prepared for combat.

*A*t first I will ask you politely:
if that doesn't work then I will tell you rudely.

*C*onformity is the best illusion for harmony.

I am in constant awe of my child's wonderment.

*L*ong ago was supposed to last forever.

*T*here is no substitute for sparring:
however, sparring must be integrated with pre-existing skills or run the
risk of extinguishing the spirit of training.

*N*owadays good customer service is like mining for gold:
when found – priceless.

*E*very life is a tale-not everyone will be told:
every life is a story – not everyone will be read:
and therein lay the rub.

*L*ove on the young is intense and razor sharp.

*T*o be hypocritical is human:
to understand that is divine.

*I*t's a fine line between monogamy and monotony.

*D*esire builds bridges reality rarely crosses.

*H*urt me with truth rather than pacify me with lies.

*M*usic makes me feel things only God could articulate.

*M*usic configures my brain to imagine things reality never produces.

*T*here is nothing more that affirms my finitude
then the parenting of my children.

*D*eath not only takes away what was but
also all of what could have been.

*P*arenting is continually feeding the mouth that bites the hand.

*E*goism is sustainment when living in a vacuum.

*W*ith Capitalism possibility only comes with feasibility.

*L*ife is a mosaic of all the moments we've lived.

*O*ne man's for-granted is another man's wish.

*M*usic is the portal by which the soul encounters heaven.

In regards to balding:
the more hair I lose the more head I get.

*S*corn is the anesthesia for pain.

*F*eelings of unexpected aliveness sometimes
exposes enslavement to regulated deadness.

*T*he simplicity of life for some can be complexing,
like the complexity of this simple phrase – "I spelt the
right word wrong and the wrong word right."

*T*hings last longer when they are in the right place.

*T*he beds we lay in don't have to be the graves we die in.

*P*sychological preservation is sometimes paid
for through physical annihilation.

*T*is not the art that maketh the master:
but the artist who is the primary factor.

*S*o we are told the universe is a caring cradle only
providing us with an infinite emptiness.

*T*read through life poetically nomadic rather
than reside in a pragmatic settlement.

*D*esign your life to be livable:
design yourself to be lovable.

*L*et the youth live young for their age will come.

*M*usic once compelled me to dream of what could be:
now music makes me grieve of what never was or will be.

A man should marry a woman he wants to fuck
and want to fuck the woman he married.

*C*ontingencies cause a reduction with certainty.

I love abnormality:
it helps me feel normal.

*T*he goal of psychotherapy is to help make the intolerable tolerable.

A "Fixer-of-others," I resolve, I am not.

*T*here's no people I want to be:
I have enough trouble being me.

*T*he slice of life is a delicious ambiguity.

*T*is those who remain that suffer the pangs of those that depart.

*W*hen reading my epitaph, remember it is
not the sum-total of who I was.

*W*e write our own eulogies for someone
else to read when we are gone.

*E*ulogies are written by the living and spoken by the remaining.

*A*ll that I am is now.

I am now.

*T*herapy is a luxury the poor can't afford.

*Y*ou can't tinker with parts of me and think you don't tamper with the whole of me.

I, man am an insatiable creature so easily dissatisfied.

*T*ransparency is poetry.

*W*hen pleasure becomes responsibility it seizes to be pleasure.

*Q*uality doesn't justify inconsistency.

*P*eople should work to improve the way they see rather than improve the way they look.

*M*y lot in life may not be a lot but it's a lot.

*T*ypically, children don't understand what they think: they interpret what they feel.

*M*ost people read quotes: only a few live them.

*L*ife is a Schizophrenic narrative played out on a Bi-Polar stage by Borderline actors.

*P*arenting at best is still noble masochism.

*I*f I sacrifice so much for others why then can't I be sacrificed to so many pleasures?

*T*he world seems a little more pure when looking into the eyes of a child.

*W*hen raising children one must learn that the days are long but the years are short.

*T*here's only so many pearls I can afford to cast before swine's before I go bankrupt.

*T*he narrative of your life is a given:
you define the genre.

*T*he narrative of one's life is a given:
the genre is yet to be determined.

*L*adies – don't fall in love with Superman:
you'll be let down by Clark Kent.
fall in love with Clark Kent and you'll be surprised by Superman.

*B*usy people want to busy people.

*I*t just is because I just am.

*F*aith provides the ability to sit in the inability to know the unknown.

*W*hen one resides amongst gladiators' disfigurement
becomes the acceptable norm.

*D*esperation sometimes causes us to abandon our mission statements.

*W*e are both – the animal that shits and the angel that soars.

*T*o give people what they want is knowledge:
to give people what they need is wisdom.

*H*e is not my son because I love him:
I love him because he is my son.

*S*ometimes we can't afford to care because
sometimes we don't feel cared for.

*S*ometimes concepts confirm our experiences and
sometimes experiences confirm our concepts.

*M*ay the death of the other cause us to love more of another.

I live today in the science fiction of my childhood.

*B*eing annoying doesn't make you funny:
it just makes you annoying.

*E*xpecting to sustain organization in a house with
children is like expecting a house of cards to remain
standing in the middle of a wind storm.

*P*aradox is the word used to describe the integration of contradictions.

*L*anguage is the human medium to best approximate reality: attempting to adorn the infinite with finite attire.

*E*xternal simplicity allows for internal complexity.

*D*on't forgo what you want just because somebody wants you.

*T*he greatness of a fight cannot be determined until that fight is fought.

*M*aybe the intention of education is to unlearn what we've learned to regain all that we've lost.

*H*igher evolution is cognitive sublimation because of biological deprivation.

*I*f Jesus was politically correct he would have never made it to the cross.

*J*ust because "you" don't know "me" doesn't mean I'm unknowable:
just because "you" don't love "me" doesn't mean I'm unlovable.

*T*he eve of everything feels eternal.

*W*hen making love use every inch:
when making love use every part:
when making love use every space.

*W*e no longer see eye-to-eye because we
no longer look at one another.

*S*ometimes we know enough to think we know more than we
really know and enough to show others we really know nothing.

*Y*ou know your growing old when the goal of the
day is to water the brown spots on your lawn.

I don't presuppose respect:
I give it to those who've earned it.

*J*ust continue being "The Shit" – some ones
bound to smell your qualities.

*B*etter a constant moving snail then an immobile cheetah.

"*L*ust" is the diagnosis of primitive biology
given by a civilized construct.

*A*utonomy is an illusion designed by those of us
who don't know how to do relationships.

*W*here does one go when it's over? When
one moves on while I still remain?

*W*e are all musical instruments waiting to be tuned
and played by the heart of a passionate musician.

*T*he world is more accessible when there is a greater trust in ourselves.

*O*h that moments were as mystical and magical as the
memories of them. Therein lay the crusade – experiencing
the moments as mystical and magical while in them.

I'm not presumptuous enough to think I can take
away pain. My hope is to reduce suffering.

*M*oral imperatives often times come from a neo-centric place (neocortex). The primitive-emotional brain is judged and held hostage by the expectations of the higher executive – (frontal-lope). The collateral damage? A bi-furcated existence.

*M*aybe women don't general like tall men:
maybe they just prefer a man taller than them.

*H*ere's an idea: No idea.
here's a thought: No thought.

*T*he unexamined life is worth living.

*I*n a multitude of counselors there is confusion.

I am not who I am because I am a therapist:
I am a therapist because of who I am.

I'm tethered to myself enough to throw caution to the wind.

*C*onsistency...thou rarest of jewels.

*T*he kiss that once was and no longer is...
is the kiss that remains... forever more.

*M*y legacy is not wrapped up in my therapy,
but in hopes of my humanity.

*J*oy is to Happiness as Kindness is to Nice.
shame is to Embarrassment as Sorrow is to Sadness.
agape is to Phileo as Shalom is to Peace.
deep comes from Deep...
deep begets Deep.

*M*ercy atones.
grace bestows.
mercy acquits.
grace gifts.

*B*etter a monogamous devil
then a cheating saint.!?

*B*etter a saint who does bad
then a devil who does good.

*J*ust because the subject sees itself outside itself
doesn't make it an objective perspective.

*A*wareness of presence
instead of thinking thoughts.

*P*arenting...the gift that keeps on taking.

I have lived many lives.
some better than others.
nonetheless...nevertheless.
they've been my life.

*T*o moral (behavioral) imperatives.
I choose an ethical obligation
to gratitude, kindness, beauty and contextualism.

*P*aradox... the intersection of contradictions.

*L*ife is a gift to be lived.
not a test to be passed.

*H*igher consciousness is the deconstructing of illusions.

*I*s it me? Seeing what I don't see?
or is it you? Seeing what you want to see?

*S*um, ergo sum.
I am, therefore I am.

*C*hildren and vacation go together like oil and water.

Printed in the United States
By Bookmasters